To

Alex

From

Ed & Amber

God's Help—
when you need Him

Promises

2

MINUTES A DAY
FOR TEENS

Promises

MINUTES A DAY

FOR TEENS

Table of Contents

Today's Promise:

INTRODUCTION:

Promises and More Promises . . . in Two Minutes a Day

God gave you a life, and now you've got to decide what to do with it. But sometimes, deciding what to do is difficult.

This little book is intended to give you a daily dose of God's promises and God's wisdom—in two minutes a day. The text is divided into 31 short devotional readings of particular interest to people who, like you, are busily engaged in life. Each chapter contains a Bible verse, a brief devotional reading, thought-provoking ideas from noted thinkers, and a prayer. The ideas on these pages will encourage you to give God your undivided attention for at least two minutes each day. But make no mistake about it: The emphasis in the previous sentence should be placed on the words "at least." In truth, you should give God lots more time than a couple of minutes a day, but hey, it's a start!

Do you have questions that you can't answer? Are you seeking to change some aspect of your life? Do you want to be a better person *and* a better Christian? If so, ask for God's help . . . starting with a regular time of devotional reading and prayer. Even two minutes is enough time to change your day . . . *and* your life.

Today's Promise:
God is Love

We know how much God loves us,
and we have put our trust in him.
God is love, and all who live in love
live in God, and God lives in them.
1 John 4:16 NLT

The Bible makes this promise: God is love. It's a sweeping statement, a profoundly important description of what God is and how God works. God's love is perfect. When we open our hearts to His perfect love, we are touched by the Creator's hand, and we are transformed.

Today, even if you can only carve out a few quiet moments, offer sincere prayers of thanksgiving to your Creator. He loves you now and throughout all eternity. Open your heart to His presence and His love.

Promises

2 MINUTES A DAY

THINK ABOUT IT

As God's children, we are the recipients of lavish love—a love that motivates us to keep trusting even when we have no idea what God is doing.
Beth Moore

The great love of God is an ocean without a bottom or a shore.
C. H. Spurgeon

Though our feelings come and go, God's love for us does not.
C. S. Lewis

The greatest love of all is God's love for us, a love that showed itself in action.
Billy Graham

GOD IS LOVE

And One More Thing . . .

> God loves each of us as if
> there were only one of us.
> **St. Augustine**

A Prayer to the Father

_ _ _ _ _ _ _ _ _ _ _ _ _ _

Lord, Your love is infinite and eternal. Although I cannot fully understand the depths of Your love, I can praise it, return it, and share it . . . today and every day. Amen

_ _ _ _ _ _ _ _ _ _ _ _ _ _

2 MINUTES A DAY

2

Today's Promise: Christ Died for You

This is how much God loved the world:
He gave his Son, his one and only Son.
And this is why: so that no one need
be destroyed; by believing in him, anyone
can have a whole and lasting life.

John 3:16 msg

Promises

Here's something to think about: Christ's love for you is personal. He loves you so much that He gave His life in order that you might spend all eternity with Him. Christ loves you individually and intimately; His is a love unbounded by time or circumstance. Are you willing to experience an intimate relationship with Him? Your Savior is waiting patiently; don't make Him wait a single minute longer. Embrace His love today. Fill yourself with the fullness of God.

THINK ABOUT IT

God proved his love on the cross.
When Christ hung, and bled, and
died, it was God saying to the world—
I love you.
Billy Graham

We will never comprehend what
it cost our Lord in physical agony
to offer His forgiveness to everyone—
no exceptions.
Anne Graham Lotz

God is my heavenly Father.
He loves me with an everlasting love.
The proof of that is the Cross.
Elisabeth Elliot

CHRIST DIED FOR YOU

A Timely Tip

Death Is a Fact of Life:

Nobody knows when or where it's going to happen to them, but death is something that everybody needs to prepare for. Why? Because death is a fact of life. So when it comes to making plans for life here on earth and for life eternal, you'd better be ready to live—and to die—right now.

A Prayer to the Father

- - - - - - - - - - - - - - - -

Lord, I'm only here on earth for a brief visit. Heaven is my real home. You've given me the gift of eternal life through Your Son Jesus. I accept Your gift, Lord. And I'll share Your Good News so that others, too, might come to know Christ's healing touch. Amen

- - - - - - - - - - - - - - - -

2 MINUTES A DAY

3

Today's Promise: When You Ask for Forgiveness . . . You Receive It

Be kind and loving to each other,
and forgive each other just as
God forgave you in Christ.
Ephesians 4:32 NCV

The Bible promises you this: When you ask God for forgiveness, He will give it. No questions asked; no explanations required.

God's power to forgive, like His love, is infinite. Despite your shortcomings, despite your sins, God offers you immediate forgiveness. It's time to take Him up on His offer.

When it comes to forgiveness, God doesn't play favorites and neither should you. You should forgive *all the people* who have harmed you (not just the people who have asked for forgiveness or the ones who have made restitution). Complete forgiveness is God's way, and it should be your way, too. Anything less is not enough.

THINK ABOUT IT

I believe that forgiveness can become
a continuing cycle: because
God forgives us, we're to forgive others;
because we forgive others,
God forgives us. Scripture presents
both parts of the cycle.
Shirley Dobson

Only the truly forgiven are truly forgiving.
C. S. Lewis

We are products of our past,
but we don't have to be prisoners of it.
God specializes in giving people
a fresh start.
Rick Warren

WHEN YOU ASK FOR FORGIVENESS . . .

Promises

And One More Thing . . .

Only God in Christ has the power
to forgive sin. But you and I must
confess it to Him personally,
specifically, and honestly
if we want to receive forgiveness.
Anne Graham Lotz

A Prayer to the Father

Dear Lord, when I ask for forgiveness,
You give it. Thank you, Father, for forgiving
me when I make mistakes. Today, I will be
quick to forgive others, just as You have
forgiven me. Amen

Today's Promise: God's Got a Plan

God is working in you to help you want to do and be able to do what pleases him.
Philippians 2:13 NCV

Promises

The Bible makes it clear: God's got a plan—a very big plan—and you're an important part of that plan. But here's the catch: God won't force His plans upon you; you've got to figure things out for yourself . . . or not.

As a follower of Christ, you should ask yourself this question: "How closely can I make my plans match God's plans?" The more closely you manage to follow the path that God intends for your life, the better.

Do you have questions or concerns about the future? Take them to God in prayer. Do you have hopes and expectations? Talk to God about your dreams. Are you carefully planning for the days and weeks ahead? Consult God as you establish your priorities. Turn every concern over to your Heavenly Father, and sincerely seek His guidance—prayerfully, earnestly, and often. Then, listen for His answers . . . and trust the answers that He gives.

2 MINUTES A DAY

THINK ABOUT IT

It's incredible to realize that what
we do each day has meaning in
the big picture of God's plan.
Bill Hybels

God has a plan for the life of every
Christian. Every circumstance,
every turn of destiny, all things work
together for your good and for His glory.
Billy Graham

God cannot lead the individual who
is not willing to give Him a blank check
with his life.
Catherine Marshall

GOD'S GOT A PLAN

Q: If God is good, why does He allow so much suffering in the world?

A: Sometimes, people do things that are foolish, impulsive, or downright evil. In those cases, it's obvious why bad stuff happens: people make it happen! But on other occasions, bad things happen, innocent people suffer, nobody is to blame, and we can't understand why. Thankfully, all our questions will be answered . . . some day. The Bible promises that when we finally get to heaven, we will understand everything. Until then, we must trust God, knowing that, in the end, He will make all things right.

A PRAYER TO THE FATHER

LORD, YOU HAVE PLANS FOR THIS WORLD AND PLANS FOR MY LIFE THAT ARE FAR GRANDER THAN I CAN IMAGINE. I WILL STUDY YOUR WORD, PRAY FOR YOUR GUIDANCE, AND SEEK YOUR WILL SO THAT *MY* LIFE MIGHT BE A TRIBUTE TO *YOUR* SON. AMEN

2 MINUTES A DAY

Today's Promise: God Can Handle It

And God, in his mighty power,
will protect you until you receive
this salvation, because
you are trusting him.
1 Peter 1:5 NLT

Promises

It's a promise that is made over and over again in the Bible: Whatever "it" is, God can handle it.

Life isn't always easy. Far from it. Sometimes, life can be very, very tough. But even then, even during our darkest moments, we're protected by a loving Heavenly Father. When we're worried, God can reassure us; when we're sad, God can comfort us. When our hearts are broken, God is not just near, He is here. So we must lift our thoughts and prayers to Him. When we do, He will answer our prayers. Why? Because He is our Shepherd, and He has promised to protect us now *and* forever.

THINK ABOUT IT

Two words will help you cope when you run low on hope: accept and trust.
Charles Swindoll

Since we're only human, understanding God is out of the question. But trusting Him is not.
Marie T. Freeman

Never be afraid to trust an unknown future to an all-knowing God.
Corrie ten Boom

Ten thousand enemies cannot stop a Christian, cannot even slow him down, if he meets them in an attitude of complete trust in God.
A. W. Tozer

GOD CAN HANDLE IT

Promises

A Timely Tip

In God We Trust? You Bet!

One of the most important lessons that you can ever learn is to trust God for everything—not some things, not most things . . . *everything!*

A Prayer to the Father

Lord, I turn this day over to You. I know that with You in charge of my life, I will be directed and protected. Thank You, God, for leading me along the path that was first walked by Your Son. Amen

2 MINUTES A DAY

6

Today's Promise:
It's a Day
Worth
Celebrating

This is the day the LORD has made.
We will rejoice and be glad in it.
Psalm 118:24 NLT

Do you feel like celebrating? If you're a believer, you should! When you allow Christ to reign over your heart, today and every day should be a time for joyful celebration.

What do you expect from the day ahead? Are you expecting God to do wonderful things, or are you living beneath a cloud of worry and doubt? The words of Psalm 118:24 remind us that every day is a gift from God. So whatever this day holds for you, begin it and end it with God as your partner and Christ as your Savior. And throughout the day, give thanks to the One who created you and saved you. God's love for you is infinite. Accept it; celebrate it; and be thankful.

THINK ABOUT IT

Nothing we do is more powerful
or more life-changing than
praising God.
Stormie Omartian

God is worthy of our praise
and is pleased when
we come before Him with thanksgiving.
Shirley Dobson

Two wings are necessary to lift
our souls toward God: prayer
and praise. Prayer asks.
Praise accepts the answer.
Mrs. Charles E. Cowman

IT'S A DAY WORTH CELEBRATING

Q: If life is a big celebration, why don't I feel like celebrating?

A: Perhaps all you need is an attitude adjustment. But if you're feeling *really* sad or *deeply* depressed, TALK ABOUT IT with people who can help, starting with your parents. Then, don't hesitate to speak with your doctor, or your pastor, or your school counselor, or all of the above. Your problem might be depression, and if it is, help is available. Ask for it. NOW!

A Prayer to the Father

Dear Lord, You have given me so many blessings, and as a way of saying "Thank You," I will celebrate. I will be a joyful Christian, Lord, quick to smile and slow to frown. And, I will share my joy with my family, my friends, and my neighbors, this day and every day. Amen

Today's Promise:
Wise Choices
Have Big
Rewards

Whoever tries to live right and
be loyal finds life, success, and honor.
Proverbs 21:21 NCV

Promises

Choices, choices, choices! You've got so many choices to make, and sometimes, making those choices isn't easy. At times you're torn between what you *want* to do and what you *ought* to do. When that happens, it's up to you to choose wisely . . . or else!

When you make wise choices, you are rewarded; when you make unwise choices, you must accept the consequences. It's as simple as that. So make sure that *your* choices are pleasing to God . . . or else!

THINK ABOUT IT

The doorstep to the temple of wisdom is a knowledge of our own ignorance.
C. H. Spurgeon

God's plan for our guidance is for us to grow gradually in wisdom before we get to the crossroads.
Bill Hybels

Do you want to be wise?
Choose wise friends.
Charles Swindoll

Knowledge can be found in books or in school. Wisdom, on the other hand, starts with God . . . and ends there.
Marie T. Freeman

WISE CHOICES HAVE BIG REWARDS

A Timely Tip

If you're not sure what to do . . .

Slow down and listen to your conscience. That little voice inside your head is remarkably dependable, but you can't depend upon it if you never listen to it. So stop, listen, and learn—your conscience is almost always right!

A Prayer to the Father

Lord, help me to make choices that are pleasing to You. Help me to be honest, patient, and kind. And above all, help me to follow the teachings of Jesus, not just today, but every day. Amen

Promises

Today's Promise:
You Can Live
Courageously

Be strong and courageous, and
do the work. Don't be afraid or
discouraged by the size of the task,
for the LORD God, my God, is with you.
He will not fail you or forsake you.
1 Chronicles 28:20 NLT

Promises

Are you trying to be a godly person in this difficult world? If so, you know it's no easy task. Ours is a time of uncertainty and danger, a time when even the most courageous fellows have legitimate cause for concern. But as believers, we can live courageously, knowing that we have been saved by a loving Father and His only begotten Son.

Sometimes, in the crush of everyday life, God may seem far away, but He is not. God is everywhere you have ever been and everywhere you will ever go. He is with you night and day; He knows your thoughts and your prayers. He is your ultimate Protector. And, when you earnestly seek His protection, you will find it because He is here—always—waiting patiently for you to reach out to Him.

2 MINUTES A DAY

THINK ABOUT IT

Do not let Satan deceive you
into being afraid of God's plans
for your life.
R. A. Torrey

Jesus Christ can make the weakest man
into a divine dreadnought,
fearing nothing.
Oswald Chambers

Faith is stronger than fear.
John Maxwell

YOU CAN LIVE COURAGEOUSLY

And One More Thing . . .

> There comes a time when we simply have to face the challenges in our lives and stop backing down.
> **John Eldredge**

A Prayer to the Father

_____

Lord, I'm only human, and sometimes I am afraid. But You are always with me, and when I turn to You, You give me courage. Let me be a courageous, faith-filled Christian, God, and keep me mindful that, with You as my protector, I am secure today... and throughout eternity. Amen

_____

Today's Promise: God Will Protect You

The ways of God are without fault.
The Lord's words are pure.
He is a shield to those who trust him.
Psalm 18:30 NCV

Promises

God has promised to protect us, and He intends to keep His promise. In a world filled with dangers and temptations, God is the ultimate armor. In a world filled with misleading messages, God's Word is the ultimate truth. In a world filled with more frustrations than we can count, God's Son offers the ultimate peace.

Will you accept God's peace and wear God's armor against the dangers of our world? Hopefully so—because when you do, you can live courageously, knowing that you possess the ultimate protection: God's unfailing love *for you*.

THINK ABOUT IT

When you are in the furnace,
your Father keeps His eye on the clock
and His hand on the thermostat.
He knows just how much we can take.
Warren Wiersbe

There is not only fear, but terrible danger,
for the life unguarded by God.
Oswald Chambers

Under heaven's lock and key,
we are protected by the most efficient
security system available:
the power of God.
Charles Swindoll

GOD WILL PROTECT YOU

Q: One of the things I'm afraid of is what other people think about me. Why am I so worried about that?

A: Misplaced priorities. You're too concerned about what people think and not concerned enough about what God thinks. Instead of worrying about what "they" think (whoever "they" are), worry more about what "He" thinks (He, of course, being God). After all, whom should you really be trying to impress—"them" or Him?

A Prayer to the Father

Lord, You have promised to protect me, and I will trust You. Today, I will live courageously as I place my hopes, my faith, and my life in Your hands. Let my life be a testimony to the transforming power of Your love, Your Grace, and Your Son. Amen

2 MINUTES A DAY

Today's Promise: Perseverance Pays

Patient endurance is what you need now,
so you will continue to do God's will.
Then you will receive all
that he has promised.
Hebrews 10:36 NLT

Promises

The Bible promises this: perseverance pays. And that's good because, as the old saying goes, "Life is a marathon, not a sprint." Because it is a marathon, life requires perseverance, so wise travelers select a traveling companion who never tires and never falters. That partner, of course, is God.

Are you tired? Ask God for strength. Are you discouraged? Believe in His promises. Are you defeated? Pray as if everything depended upon God, and work as if everything depended upon yourself. With God's help, you can persevere . . . and you will.

THINK ABOUT IT

Failure is one of life's most powerful
teachers. How we handle our failures
determines whether we're going to
simply "get by" in life or "press on."
Beth Moore

By perseverance, the snail reached the ark.
C. H. Spurgeon

Stand still and refuse to retreat. Look at it
as God looks at it and draw upon
his power to hold up under the blast.
Charles Swindoll

All rising to a great place is
by a winding stair.
Francis Bacon

PERSEVERANCE PAYS

Promises

Q: I'm pretty sure things aren't going to work out, so why shouldn't I go ahead and quit now?

A: Because things change, and that includes your problems. Even if you are unable to see a solution today, you may spot one tomorrow, so don't give up, even if you're discouraged.

A Prayer to the Father

Lord, some days I feel like there's no way I can win. But when I'm discouraged, let me turn to You for strength, courage, and faith. When I find my strength in You, Lord, I am protected, today and forever. Amen

Today's Promise:
Joy Can Be Yours . . . Today

Shout with joy to the LORD, O earth!
Worship the LORD with gladness.
Come before him, singing with joy.
Psalm 100:1, 2 NLT

When will you rejoice at God's marvelous creation: today or tomorrow? When will you accept His abundance: now or later? When will you accept the joy that can and should be yours: in the present moment or in the distant future? The answer, of course, is straightforward: The best moment to accept God's gifts is the present one.

Will you accept God's blessings now or later? Are you willing to give Him your full attention today? Hopefully so. He deserves it. And so, for that matter, do you.

THINK ABOUT IT

To praise God is to please God.
Jim Gallery

Most of the verses written about praise in
God's Word were voiced by people
faced with crushing heartaches,
injustice, treachery, slander,
and scores of other difficult situations.
Joni Eareckson Tada

Praise is the highest occupation
of any being.
Max Lucado

JOY CAN BE YOURS ... TODAY

And One More Thing . . .

The time for universal praise is sure
to come some day.
Let us begin to do our part now.
Hannah Whitall Smith

A Prayer to the Father

Lord, make me a joyous Christian.
Because of my salvation through Your Son,
I have every reason to celebrate life. Let me
share the joyful news of Jesus Christ, and
let my life be a testimony to His love and
to His grace. Amen

12

Today's Promise: Kindness is Rewarded

Kind people do themselves a favor,
but cruel people bring trouble
on themselves.
Proverbs 11:17 NCV

Promises

If we believe the words of Proverbs 11:17—and we should—then we understand that kindness is its own reward. And, if we to obey the commandments of our Savior—and we should—we must sow seeds of kindness wherever we go.

Kindness, compassion, and forgiveness are hallmarks of our Christian faith. So today, in honor of the One who first showed compassion for us, let's teach our families and friends the art of kindness through our words and through our deeds. Our loved ones are watching . . . and so is God.

2 MINUTES A DAY

THINK ABOUT IT

When you extend hospitality to others,
you're not trying to impress people,
you're trying to reflect God to them.
Max Lucado

A little kindly advice is better than
a great deal of scolding.
Fanny Crosby

Be so preoccupied with good will
that you haven't room for ill will.
E. Stanley Jones

Keep your eyes open wide and
your heart open wider.
Criswell Freeman

KINDNESS IS REWARDED

Promises

What God Has To Say About It

Finally, all of you should be of
one mind, full of sympathy toward
each other, loving one another
with tender hearts
and humble minds.
1 Peter 3:8 NLT

A Prayer to the Father

Lord, make me a loving, encouraging Christian. And, let my love for Christ be reflected through the kindness that I show to those who need the healing touch of the Master's hand. Amen

2 MINUTES A DAY

13

Today's Promise: Tough Times Don't Last

I took my troubles to the LORD;
I cried out to him, and
he answered my prayer.
Psalm 120:1 NLT

Promises

The Bible promises this: tough times are temporary but God's love is not— God's love lasts forever. So what does that mean to you? Just this: From time to time, everybody faces tough times, and so will you. And when tough times arrive, God will always stand ready to protect you *and* heal you.

Psalm 147 promises, "He heals the brokenhearted" (v. 3 NIV), but Psalm 147 *doesn't* say that He heals them instantly. Usually, it takes time (and maybe even a little help from you) for God to fix things. So, if you're facing tough times, face them with God by your side. If you find yourself in any kind of trouble, pray about it and ask God for help. And be patient. God will work things out, just as He has promised, but He will do it in His own way and in His own time.

THINK ABOUT IT

Jesus does not say, "There is no storm."
He says, "I am here, do not toss, but trust."
Vance Havner

Let's thank God for allowing us
to experience troubles that drive us
closer to Him.
Shirley Dobson

Remember, we go through nothing
that God does not know about.
Oswald Chambers

God will lead you through, not around,
the valley of the shadow of death.
Max Lucado

TOUGH TIMES DON'T LAST

A Timely Tip

Talk about it . . .

If you're having tough times, don't hit the panic button and don't keep everything bottled up inside. Find a person you can really trust, and talk things over. A second opinion (or, for that matter, a third, fourth, or fifth opinion) is usually helpful.

A Prayer to the Father

Lord, sometimes life is so difficult that I can't see any hope for the future. But with You, there is always hope. Today, I will keep Your promises in my heart, and I will faithfully trust the future to You. Amen

Promises

Today's Promise: God's Grace is a Gift

For by grace you have been saved
through faith, and that not of yourselves;
it is the gift of God.
Ephesians 2:8 NKJV

Here's the great news: God's grace is not earned . . . and thank goodness it's not! If God's grace were some sort of reward for good behavior, none of us could earn enough brownie points to win the big prize. But it doesn't work that way. Grace is a free offer from God. By accepting that offer, we transform our lives today and forever.

God's grace is not just any old gift; it's the ultimate gift, and we owe Him our eternal gratitude. Our Heavenly Father is waiting patiently for each of us to accept His Son and receive His grace. Let us accept that gift today so that we might enjoy God's presence now and throughout all eternity.

THINK ABOUT IT

Abounding sin is the terror of the world,
but abounding grace is the hope
of mankind.
A. W. Tozer

How beautiful it is to learn that grace
isn't fragile, and that in the family of God
we can fail and not be a failure.
Gloria Gaither

We will never cease to need our Father—
His wisdom, direction, help, and support.
We will never outgrow Him.
We will always need His grace.
Kay Arthur

GOD'S GRACE IS A GIFT

Promises

And One More Thing . . .

> If we only believe and ask,
> a full measure of God's grace
> is available to any of us.
> **Charles Swindoll**

A Prayer to the Father

Accepting Your grace can be hard, Lord. Somehow, I feel that I must earn Your love and Your acceptance. Yet, the Bible promises that You love me and saved me by Your grace. It is a gift I can only accept and cannot earn. Thank You for Your priceless, everlasting gift. Amen

2 MINUTES A DAY

Today's Promise: When You Stop Judging, You Win

Stop judging others, and you will not
be judged. Stop criticizing others, or
it will all come back on you.
If you forgive others, you will be forgiven.
Luke 6:37 NLT

Promises

Here's something worth thinking about: If you judge other people harshly, God will judge you in the same fashion. But that's not all (thank goodness). The Bible also promises that if you forgive others, you, too, will be forgiven.

Have you developed the bad habit of behaving like an amateur judge and jury, assigning blame and condemnation wherever you go? If so, it's time to grow up and obey God. When it comes to judging everything and everybody, God doesn't need your help.

THINK ABOUT IT

Jesus is the only One Who makes
not only our sins but also the sins
of others against us forgivable.
Anne Graham Lotz

Doing an injury puts you below
your enemy; revenging an injury makes
you even with him; forgiving
an injury sets you above him!
Anonymous

Only the truly forgiven are truly forgiving.
C. S. Lewis

WHEN YOU STOP JUDGING, YOU WIN

Promises

Q: What if it's really hard for me to stop judging people?

A: If it were easy, everybody would be doing it—but it's not. We human beings are hard-wired with the tendency to blame, to judge, to gossip, and to criticize. And if some of those words describe *your* behavior, pray about it . . . and keep praying about it . . . until God helps you correct those bad habits.

A Prayer to the Father

Lord, it's so easy to judge other people, but it's also easy to misjudge them. Only You can judge a human heart, Lord, so let me love my friends and neighbors, and let me help them, but never let me judge them. Amen

16

Today's Promise: When You Ask, You Receive

Ask, and God will give to you. Search, and you will find. Knock, and the door will open for you. Yes, everyone who asks will receive. Everyone who searches will find. And everyone who knocks will have the door opened.

Matthew 7:7, 8 NCV

Promises

Matthew 7:7, 8 makes a promise that God intends to keep: When you pray earnestly, fervently, and often, He will answer your prayers. And if you're willing to pray for big things, He will answer those prayers, too.

Too many people, however, are too timid or too pessimistic to ask God to do big things. Don't count yourself among their number.

God can *and will* do great things through you *if* you have the courage to ask Him and the determination to keep asking Him. Honor God by making big requests. But don't expect Him to do all the work. When *you* do your part, *He* will do His part.

THINK ABOUT IT

Prayer keeps us in constant communion
with God, which is the goal of
our entire believing lives.
Beth Moore

History has been changed time after time
because of prayer. I tell you,
history could be changed again if people
went to their knees in believing prayer.
Billy Graham

There are some forms of spiritual life
which are not absolutely essential, but
prayer is the very essence of spirituality.
C. H. Spurgeon

WHEN YOU ASK, YOU RECEIVE.

Promises

And One More Thing . . .

When you ask God to do something,
don't ask timidly;
put your whole heart into it.
Marie T. Freeman

A Prayer to the Father

————————————————

Lord, today I will ask You for the things I need. In every situation, I will come to You in prayer. You know what I want, Lord, and more importantly, You know what I need. Yet even though I know that You know, I still won't be too timid—or too busy—to ask. Amen

————————————————

17

Today's Promise: Hard Work Pays

But as for you, be strong and
do not give up,
for your work will be rewarded.
2 Chronicles 15:7 NIV

God has work for you to do, but He won't make you do it. Since the days of Adam and Eve, God has allowed His children to make choices for themselves, and so it is with you. You've got choices to make . . . lots of them. If you choose wisely, you'll be rewarded; if you choose unwisely, you'll bear the consequences.

Whether you're in school or in the workplace, your success will depend, in large part, upon the quality and quantity of your work. God has created a world in which diligence is rewarded and sloth is not. So whatever you choose to do, do it with commitment, excitement, and vigor.

God did not create you for a life of mediocrity; He created you for far greater things. Reaching for greater things usually requires work and lots of it, which is perfectly fine with God. After all, He knows that you're up to the task, and He has big plans for you. Very big plans.

THINK ABOUT IT

"They that sow bountifully shall reap
also bountifully," is as true
in spiritual things as in material.
Lottie Moon

Ordinary work, which is what most of us
do most of the time, is ordained by God
every bit as much as is the extraordinary.
Elisabeth Elliot

It may be that the day of judgment
will dawn tomorrow; in that case,
we shall gladly stop working
for a better tomorrow. But not before.
Dietrich Bonhoeffer

HARD WORK PAYS

A Timely Tip

Have Faith and Get Busy:

Here's a time-tested formula for success: have faith in God and do the work. Remember: There are no shortcuts to any place worth going.

A Prayer to the Father

Lord, let me be an diligent worker in Your fields. Those fields are ripe, Lord, and Your workers are few. Let me be counted as Your faithful, hard-working servant today, and every day. Amen

Today's Promise: God's Timing is Perfect

He has made everything beautiful in its time. He has also set eternity in the hearts of men; yet they cannot fathom what God has done from beginning to end.

Ecclesiastes 3:11 NIV

Promises

We human beings are *so* impatient. We know what we want, and we know exactly when we want it: RIGHT NOW! But, God knows better. He has created a world that unfolds according to His own timetable, not ours. And that's good, because God's plans are perfect (while our plans most certainly are not).

As Christians, we must be patient as we wait for God to show us the wonderful things that He has in store for us. And while we're waiting for God to make His plans clear, let's keep praying and keep giving thanks to the One who has given us more blessings than we can count.

THINK ABOUT IT

Waiting on God brings us to
the journey's end quicker than our feet.
Mrs. Charles E. Cowman

God's silence is in no way indicative of
His activity or involvement in our lives.
He may be silent, but He is not still.
Charles Swindoll

Will not the Lord's time be better
than your time?
C. H. Spurgeon

GOD'S TIMING IS PERFECT

A Timely Tip

Trust God's Timing.

Remember: God's timing is best, so don't allow yourself to become discouraged if things don't work out exactly as you wish. Instead of worrying about your future, entrust it to God. He knows exactly what you need and exactly when you need it.

A Prayer to the Father

Lord, my sense of timing is imperfect; Yours is not. Let me trust in Your timetable for my life, and give me the patience and the wisdom to trust Your plans, not my own. Amen

19

Today's Promise:
God Guides

The LORD says, "I will guide you along
the best pathway for your life.
I will advise you and watch over you."
Psalm 32:8 NLT

The Bible promises that God will guide you *if* you let Him. Your job, of course, is to let Him. But sometimes, you will be tempted to do otherwise. Sometimes, you'll be tempted to go along with the crowd; other times, you'll be tempted to do things your way, not God's way. When you feel those temptations, resist them.

What will you allow to guide you through the coming day: your own desires (or, for that matter, the desires of your friends)? Or will you allow God to lead the way? The answer should be obvious. You should let God be your guide. When you entrust your life to Him completely and without reservation, God will give you the strength to meet any challenge, the courage to face any trial, and the wisdom to live in His righteousness. So trust Him today and seek His guidance. When you do, your next step will be the right one.

THINK ABOUT IT

God's guidance is even more important
than common sense. I can declare that
the deepest darkness is outshone
by the light of Jesus.
Corrie ten Boom

We have ample evidence that the Lord is
able to guide. The promises cover every
imaginable situation. All we need to do
is to take the hand He stretches out.
Elisabeth Elliot

If we want to hear God's voice,
we must surrender our minds
and hearts to Him.
Billy Graham

GOD GUIDES

Promises

And One More Thing . . .

Only He can guide you to invest
your life in worthwhile ways.
This guidance will come
as you "walk" with Him
and listen to Him.
Henry Blackaby and Claude King

A Prayer to the Father

Dear Lord, You are my Teacher and my Guide.
Help me to learn from You. And then, let me show
others what it means to be a kind, generous, loving
Christian. Amen

2 MINUTES A DAY

20

Today's Promise:
Friendship is as Friendship Does

A friend loves you all the time,
and a brother helps in time of trouble.
Proverbs 17:17 NCV

Genuine friendship should be treasured and nourished. How? The surest way is by observing the Golden Rule.

As Christians, we are governed by the Golden Rule: We are commanded to treat others as we wish to be treated. And when we treat others with kindness, courtesy, and respect, we build friendships that can last a lifetime.

Throughout the Bible, we are reminded to love one another and care for one another. In other words, the Bible teaches us that friendship is as friendship does.

Do you want to have great friends? Then be one. And make no mistake: That's exactly the kind of friend that God wants you to be.

THINK ABOUT IT

Insomuch as any one pushes you nearer
to God, he or she is your friend.
Anonymous

A person who really cares about his
or her neighbor, a person who genuinely
loves others, is a person who
bears witness to the truth.
Anne Graham Lotz

Yes, the Spirit was sent to be our Counselor.
Yes, Jesus speaks to us personally.
But often He works through
another human being.
John Eldredge

In friendship, God opens your eyes
to the glories of Himself.
Joni Eareckson Tada

FRIENDSHIP IS AS FRIENDSHIP DOES

Promises

Q: I want to make more friends. How can I do it?

A: Try this: First, become more interested in them . . . and pretty soon they'll become more interested in you!

A Prayer to the Father

Lord, thank You for my friends. Let me be a trustworthy friend to others, and let my love for You be reflected in my genuine love for them. Amen

21

Today's Promise: God Loves a Cheerful Giver

Each person should do as he has decided in his heart—not out of regret or out of necessity, for God loves a cheerful giver.

2 Corinthians 9:7 HCSB

Are you a cheerful giver? If you intend to obey God's commandments, you must be. When you give, God looks not only at the quality of your gift, but also at the condition of your heart. If you give generously, joyfully, and without complaint, you obey God's Word. But, if you make your gifts grudgingly, or if the motivation for your gift is selfish, you disobey your Creator, *even* if you have tithed in accordance with Biblical principles.

Today, take God's commandments to heart and make this pledge: Be a cheerful, generous, and courageous giver. The world needs your help, and you need the spiritual rewards that will be yours when you give faithfully, prayerfully, and cheerfully.

THINK ABOUT IT

In the kingdom of God, the surest way
to lose something is to try to protect it,
and the best way to keep it is to let it go.
A. W. Tozer

The test of generosity is not how much
you give, but how much you have left.
Anonymous

Selfishness is as far from Christianity
as darkness is from light.
C. H. Spurgeon

It is the duty of every Christian
to be Christ to his neighbor.
Martin Luther

GOD LOVES A CHEERFUL GIVER

Q: Would you like to be a happier Person?

A: Then think about this: The Bible says that if you become a more generous person, you'll become a happier person, too. Try reading Psalm 41:1.

A Prayer to the Father

——————————————

Lord, make me a generous and cheerful Christian. Let me be kind to those who need my encouragement, and let me share with those who need my help, today and every day. Amen

——————————————

Today's Promise: God Has Given You Special Gifts

God has given gifts to each of you from his great variety of spiritual gifts. Manage them well so that God's generosity can flow through you.
1 Peter 4:10 NLT

Promises

It's a fact: You've got special talents that need to be refined. All people possess special gifts—gifts from God—and you are no exception. But, your gift is no guarantee of success; it must be cultivated—by you—or it will go unused . . . and God's gift to you will be squandered.

Today, nurture those talents that God has given to you. Then, share your gifts with the world. After all, the best way to say "Thank You" for God's gifts is to use them.

THINK ABOUT IT

In the great orchestra we call life,
you have an instrument and a song,
and you owe it to God to play them
both sublimely.

Max Lucado

You are the only person on earth
who can use your ability.

Zig Ziglar

What we are is God's gift to us.
What we become is our gift to God.

Anonymous

GOD HAS GIVEN YOU SPECIAL GIFTS

And One More Thing . . .

> God often reveals His direction
> for our lives through the way
> He made us . . . with a certain
> personality and unique skills.
> **Bill Hybels**

A Prayer to the Father

Lord, thank You for the talents You have given me. Let me treasure them and use them for Your glory as I walk in the footsteps of Your Son. Amen

----

Promises

23

Today's Promise: God Gives Strength

The Lord is my light and my salvation;
whom shall I fear?
The Lord is the strength of my life;
Of whom shall I be afraid?

Psalm 27:1 NKJV

Promises

Where do you go to find strength? The gym? The health food store? The expresso bar? There's a better source of strength, of course, and that source is God. He is a never-ending source of strength and courage if you call upon Him.

Have you "tapped in" to the power of God? Have you turned your life and your heart over to Him, or are you muddling along under your own power? The answer to this question will determine the quality of your life here on earth and the destiny of your life throughout all eternity. So start tapping in—and remember that when it comes to strength, God is the Ultimate Source.

THINK ABOUT IT

When God is our strength,
it is strength indeed; when our strength
is our own, it is only weakness.
St. Augustine

If we take God's program,
we can have God's power—
not otherwise.
E. Stanley Jones

The strength that we claim from
God's Word does not depend on
circumstances. Circumstances will be
difficult, but our strength will be sufficient.
Corrie ten Boom

GOD GIVES STRENGTH

What God Has To Say About It

> But those who wait on the LORD
> will find new strength.
> They will fly high on wings like eagles.
> They will run and not grow weary.
> They will walk and not faint.
> **Isaiah 40:31** NLT

A Prayer to the Father

Dear Lord, I will turn to You for strength. When my responsibilities seem overwhelming, I will trust You to give me courage and perspective. Today and every day, I will look to You as the ultimate source of my hope, my strength, my peace, and my salvation. Amen

24

Today's Promise: God Will Bless You Abundantly

I have come that they may have life,
and that they may have it
more abundantly.
John 10:10 NKJV

God sent His Son so that mankind might enjoy the abundant life that Jesus describes in the words of John 10:10. But, God's gifts are not guaranteed; they must be claimed by those who choose to follow Christ.

What is your focus today? Are you focused on God's Word and His will for your life? Or are you focused on the distractions of a difficult, temptation-filled world? If you sincerely seek the spiritual abundance that your Savior offers, then you should follow Him completely and without reservation. When you do, you will receive the love, the life, and the abundance that He has promised.

THINK ABOUT IT

People, places, and things were
never meant to give us life.
God alone is the author of a fulfilling life.
Gary Smalley & John Trent

Jesus wants Life for us, Life with a capital L.
John Eldredge

The Bible says that being a Christian is
not only a great way to die,
but it's also the best way to live.
Bill Hybels

If we were given all we wanted here,
our hearts would settle for
this world rather than the next.
Elisabeth Elliot

GOD WILL BLESS YOU ABUNDANTLY

Promises

Q: When Jesus talked about "abundance," was He talking about "money"?

A: Nope. When Christ talked about abundance, He was concerned with people's spiritual well-being, not their financial well-being. And come to think of it, that's what *you* should be concerned about, too!

A Prayer to the Father

Dear Lord, You have offered me the gift of abundance through Your Son. Thank You, Father, for the abundant life that is mine through Christ Jesus. Let me accept His gifts and use them to glorify You. Amen

2 MINUTES A DAY

25

Today's Promise: Prayer is Powerful

When a believing person prays,
great things happen.
James 5:16 NCV

Promises

The Bible promises that prayer is powerful . . . *very* powerful. So, prayer is not a thing to be taken lightly or to be used infrequently.

Is prayer an integral part of your daily life, or is it a hit-or-miss habit? Do you "pray without ceasing," or is your prayer life an afterthought? The quality of your spiritual life will be in direct proportion to the quality of your prayer life, so conduct yourself accordingly.

Prayer changes things, *and* it changes you. So don't limit your prayers to meals or to bedtime. Pray constantly about things great and small. God is listening, and He wants to hear from you now.

THINK ABOUT IT

Prayer is never the least we can do;
it is always the most!
A. W. Tozer

O, let the place of secret prayer become
to me the most beloved spot on earth.
Andrew Murray

Prayer moves the arm that moves
the world.
Annie Armstrong

Pray as if it's all up to God,
work as if it's all up to you.
Anonymous

PRAYER IS POWERFUL

Promises

A Timely Tip

Sometimes, the Answer Is "No":

God does not answer all of our prayers in the affirmative, nor should He. His job is not to grant all our earthly requests; His job is to offer us eternal salvation (for which we must be eternally grateful). When we are disappointed by the realities of life here on earth, we should remember that our prayers are always answered by a sovereign, all-knowing God, and that we must trust Him, whether He answers "Yes", "No", or "Not yet".

A Prayer to the Father

Lord, make me a prayerful Christian. In good times and in bad times, in whatever state I find myself, let me turn my prayers to You. You always hear my prayers, God; let me always pray them! Amen

Today's Promise:
Praise Pays

Praise the Lord!
Happy are those who respect the Lord,
who want what he commands.
Psalm 112:1 NCV

The Bible makes it clear: it pays to praise God. But sometimes, we allow ourselves to become so preoccupied with the demands of everyday life that we forget to say "Thank You" to the Giver of all good gifts.

Worship and praise should be a part of everything we do. Otherwise, we quickly lose perspective as we fall prey to the demands of the moment.

Do you sincerely desire to be a worthy servant of the One who has given you eternal love and eternal life? Then praise Him for who He is and for what He has done for you. And don't just praise Him on Sunday morning. Praise Him all day long, every day, for as long as you live . . . and then for all eternity.

THINK ABOUT IT

Nothing we do is more powerful or more life-changing than praising God.
Stormie Omartian

God is worthy of our praise and is pleased when we come before Him with thanksgiving.
Shirley Dobson

Praise—lifting up our heart and hands, exulting with our voices, singing His praises—is the occupation of those who dwell in the kingdom.
Max Lucado

PRAISE PAYS

Promises

A Timely Tip

Praise Him!

One of the main reasons you need to go to church is to praise God. But, you need not wait until Sunday rolls around to thank your Heavenly Father. Instead, you can praise Him many times each day by saying silent prayers that only He can hear.

A Prayer to the Father

Dear Lord, today and every day I will praise You. I will come to You with hope in my heart and words of gratitude on my lips. Let me follow in the footsteps of Your Son, and let my thoughts, my prayers, my words, and my deeds praise You now and forever. Amen

Today's Promise:
Discipline
Pays
Dividends

He did it with all his heart.
So he prospered.
2 Chronicles 31:21 NKJV

Promises

God's Word is clear: As believers, we are called to lead lives of discipline, diligence, moderation, and maturity. But the world often tempts us to behave otherwise. Everywhere we turn, or so it seems, we are faced with powerful temptations to behave in undisciplined, ungodly ways.

We live in a world in which leisure is glorified and misbehavior is glamorized. But God has other plans.

Life's greatest rewards seldom fall into our laps; to the contrary, God rewards diligence and righteousness just as certainly as He punishes laziness and sin. As believers in a just God, we should behave accordingly.

2 MINUTES A DAY

THINK ABOUT IT

The alternative to discipline is disaster.
Vance Havner

True will power and courage are not on
the battlefield, but in everyday conquests
over our inertia, laziness, and boredom.
D. L. Moody

If one examines the secret behind
a championship football team,
a magnificent orchestra, or
a successful business, the principal
ingredient is invariably discipline.
James Dobson

God does not discipline us to subdue us,
but to condition us for a life
of usefulness and blessedness.
Billy Graham

DISCIPLINE PAYS DIVIDENDS

A Timely Tip

A disciplined lifestyle gives you more control:

The more disciplined you become, the more you can take control over your life (which, by the way, is far better than letting your life take control over you).

A Prayer to the Father

Lord, I want to be a disciplined believer. Let me use my time wisely, and let me teach others by the faithfulness of my conduct, today and every day. Amen

Today's Promise: God's Word Offers Wisdom

Only the Lord gives wisdom;
he gives knowledge and understanding
Proverbs 2:6 NCV

Promises

If you look it up in a dictionary, you'll see that the word "wisdom" means "using good judgement, and knowing what is true." But there's more: It's not just enough to *know* what's right; if you really want to become a wise person, you must also *do* what's right.

The ultimate source of wisdom, of course, is the Word of God. When you study God's Word and live according to His commandments, you will accumulate wisdom day by day. And finally, with God's help, you'll have enough wisdom to keep and enough left over to share.

THINK ABOUT IT

Wise people listen to wise instruction,
especially instruction from
the Word of God.
Warren Wiersbe

If you lack knowledge, go to school.
If you lack wisdom, get on your knees.
Vance Havner

The Bible is God's Word, given to us
by God Himself so we can know Him
and His will for our lives.
Billy Graham

The more wisdom enters our hearts,
the more we will be able to trust
our hearts in difficult situations.
John Eldredge

GOD'S WORD OFFERS WISDOM

Q: Need wisdom?

A: Then start hanging out with wise people. Sometimes, it may be a friend, but don't overlook your parents .

A Prayer to the Father

_ _ _ _ _ _ _ _ _ _ _ _ _ _ _

Lord, when I trust in the wisdom of the world, I will sometimes be led astray, but when I trust in Your wisdom, I build my life on a firm foundation. Today and every day I will trust Your Word and follow it, knowing that the ultimate wisdom is Your wisdom and the ultimate truth is Your truth. Amen

_ _ _ _ _ _ _ _ _ _ _ _ _ _ _

Today's Promise:
God is Here

Be still, and know that I am God.
Psalm 46:10 NKJV

Do you ever wonder if God is really listening? If so, you're not the first person to think such thoughts. In fact, some of the biggest heroes in the Bible had their doubts—and so, perhaps, will you. But when questions arise and doubts begin to creep into your mind, remember this: God hasn't gone on vacation, and He doesn't have an unlisted number. You can talk with Him any time you feel like it. In fact, He's right here, right now, listening to your thoughts and prayers, watching over your every move.

Sometimes, you will allow yourself to become *very* busy, and that's when you may be tempted to ignore God. But, when you quiet yourself long enough to acknowledge His presence, God will touch your heart and restore your spirits. By the way, He's ready to talk right now. Are you?

THINK ABOUT IT

We look for visions of heaven,
but we never dream that, all the time,
God is in the commonplace things
and people around us.
Oswald Chambers

The next time your hear a baby laugh
or see an ocean wave, take note.
Pause and listen as His Majesty whispers
ever so gently, "I'm here."
Max Lucado

No matter what trials we face,
Christ never leaves us.
Billy Graham

We need never shout across the spaces to
an absent God. He is nearer than our own
soul, closer than our most secret thoughts.
A. W. Tozer

GOD IS HERE

A Timely Tip

Want to talk to God?
Then don't make Him shout.

If you really want to hear from God, go to a quiet place and listen. If you keep listening long enough and carefully enough, He'll start talking.

A Prayer to the Father

Lord, in the quiet moments of this day, I will turn my thoughts and prayers to You. In these silent moments, I will sense Your presence, and I will seek Your will for my life, knowing that when I accept Your peace, I will be blessed today and throughout eternity. Amen

30

Today's Promise: Spiritual Growth Can Last a Lifetime

Grow in grace and understanding
of our Master and Savior, Jesus Christ.
Glory to the Master, now and forever! Yes!

2 Peter 3:18 MSG

Are you about as mature as you're ever going to be? Hopefully not! When it comes to your faith, God doesn't intend for you to become "fully grown," at least not in *this* lifetime.

As a Christian, you should continue to grow in the love and the knowledge of your Savior as long as you live. How? By studying God's Word, by obeying His commandments, and by allowing His Son to reign over your heart.

Are you continually seeking to become a more mature believer? Hopefully so, because that's exactly what you owe to God *and* to yourself.

THINK ABOUT IT

If we do not deal with sin,
our spiritual lives become stagnant
and we lose our attractiveness
and usefulness to God.
Anne Graham Lotz

Often God shuts a door in our face so
that He can open the door through
which He wants us to go.
Catherine Marshall

The Scriptures were not given for
our information, but for our transformation.
D. L. Moody

There is wonderful freedom and
joy in coming to recognize that
the fun is in the becoming.
Gloria Gaither

SPIRITUAL GROWTH CAN LAST A LIFETIME

Promises

Q: How do I know if I can still keep growing as a Christian?

A: Check your pulse. If it's still beating, then you can still keep growing. You can *never* have enough faith or knowledge.

A Prayer to the Father

— — — — — — — — — — — — — — -

Lord, help me to keep growing spiritually and emotionally. Let me live according to Your Word, and let me grow in my faith every day that I live. Amen

— — — — — — — — — — — — — — -

31

Today's Promise: With God, Anything is Possible

All things are possible for the one
who believes.
Mark 9:23 NCV

Jesus taught His disciples that if they had faith, they could move mountains. You can too. If you place your faith, your trust, indeed your life in the hands of Christ Jesus, you'll be amazed at the marvelous things He can do with you and through you. Faith is a willingness to believe in things that are unseeable and to trust in things that are unknowable.

Today and every day, strengthen your faith through praise, through worship, through Bible study, and through prayer. God has big plans for you, so trust His plans and strengthen your faith in Him. With God, all things are possible, and He stands ready to help you accomplish miraculous things with your life . . . *if* you have faith.

THINK ABOUT IT

When Jesus is in our midst, He brings His limitless power along as well. But, Jesus must be in the middle, all eyes and hearts focused on Him.

Shirley Dobson

The God who spoke still speaks. He comes into our world. He comes into your world. He comes to do what you can't.

Max Lucado

God never has to scratch His head. He is always in sovereign control.

Charles Swindoll

WITH GOD, ANYTHING IS POSSIBLE

A Timely Tip

Focus on Possibilities, Not Roadblocks:

The road of life contains a number of potholes and stumbling blocks. Of course, you will encounter them from time to time. But, don't invest large quantities of your life focusing on past misfortunes. On the road of life, regret is a dead end.

A Prayer to the Father

Lord, for You, nothing is impossible. Let me trust in Your power to do the miraculous, and let me trust in Your willingness to work miracles in my life—and in my heart. Amen

Promises

More Good Stuff

Quotations and Bible Verses by Topic

Friendship

As iron sharpens iron,
a friend sharpens a friend.
Proverbs 27:17 NLT

A friend is one who makes me
do my best.
Oswald Chambers

Don't bypass the potential for meaningful
friendships just because of differences.
Explore them. Embrace them.
Love them.
Luci Swindoll

Do you want to be wise?
Choose wise friends.
Charles Swindoll

School

It is not good to have zeal without
knowledge, nor to be hasty
and miss the way.
Proverbs 19:2 NIV

The Bible calls for discipline and
a recognition of authority.
Children must learn this at home.
Billy Graham

If one examines the secret behind
a championship football team,
a magnificent orchestra, or
a successful business, the principal
ingredient is invariably discipline.
James Dobson

MORE GOOD STUFF

Promises

Tough Times

But I will call on God, and the LORD
will rescue me. Morning, noon,
and night I plead aloud in my distress,
and the LORD hears my voice.
Psalm 55:16, 17 NLT

When you are in the furnace, your Father
keeps His eye on the clock and His hand
on the thermostat. He knows just how
much you can take.
Warren Wiersbe

Let's thank God for allowing us to
experience troubles that drive us closer to
Him.
Shirley Dobson

2 MINUTES A DAY

Jesus does not say, "There is no storm." He says, "I am here, do not toss, but trust."

Vance Havner

My Speech

Watch the way you talk. Let nothing
foul or dirty come out of your mouth.
Say only what helps, each word a gift.
Ephesians 4:29 msg

Fill the heart with the love of Christ so
that only truth and purity can
come out of the mouth.
Warren Wiersbe

The great test of a man's character
is his tongue.
Oswald Chambers

When you talk, choose the very same
words that you would use if Jesus were
looking over your shoulder. Because He is.
Marie T. Freeman

Self-Esteem

Happy is he who does not
condemn himself....
Romans 14:22 NKJV

Being loved by Him whose opinion matters
most gives us the security to risk loving,
too—even loving ourselves.
Gloria Gaither

As you and I lay up for ourselves living,
lasting treasures in Heaven, we come
to the awesome conclusion that
we ourselves are His treasure!
Anne Graham Lotz

Find satisfaction in Him who made you,
and only then find satisfaction
in yourself as part of His creation.
St. Augustine

MORE GOOD STUFF

God's Love

But God demonstrates His own love
toward us, in that while we were
still sinners, Christ died for us.
Romans 5:8 NKJV

Everything I possess of any worth is
a direct product of God's love.
Beth Moore

God loves you and wants you
to experience peace and life—
abundant and eternal.
Billy Graham

After ten thousand insults,
He still loves you as infinitely as ever.
C. H. Spurgeon

2 MINUTES A DAY

Respecting my Parents

Children, obey your parents in the Lord,
for this is right.
Ephesians 6:1 NIV

If you are willing to honor a person out
of respect for God, you can be assured
that God will honor you.
Beth Moore

Homes that are built on anything other
than love are bound to crumble.
Billy Graham

There is always room for more loving
forgiveness within our homes.
James Dobson

MORE GOOD STUFF

Fear

In my anguish I cried to the LORD,
and he answered by setting me free.
The LORD is with me; I will not be afraid.
What can man do to me?
Psalm 118:5, 6 NIV

Jesus came treading the waves; and
so he puts all the swelling tumults of life
under his feet. Christians—why afraid?
St. Augustine

Fear is a self-imposed prison that will
keep you from becoming what
God intends for you to be.
Rick Warren

2 MINUTES A DAY

Sadness

"For my thoughts are not your thoughts,
neither are your ways my ways," declares
the LORD. "You will go out in joy and
be led forth in peace; the mountains and
hills will burst into song before you, and all
the trees of the field will clap their hands."
Isaiah 55:8, 12 NIV

Just as courage is faith in good,
so discouragement is faith in evil, and,
while courage opens the door to good,
discouragement opens it to evil.
Hannah Whitall Smith

What is the cure for disillusionment?
Putting our complete hope and
trust in the living Lord.
Charles Swindoll

MORE GOOD STUFF

Forgiveness

And be ye kind one to another,
tenderhearted, forgiving one another,
even as God for Christ's sake
hath forgiven you.
Ephesians 4:32 KJV

Learning how to forgive and forget is one
of the secrets of a happy Christian life.
Warren Wiersbe

Our Lord worked with people as
they were, and He was patient—
not tolerant of sin, but compassionate.
Vance Havner

The love of God is revealed in that
He laid down His life for His enemies.
Oswald Chambers

2 MINUTES A DAY

Anger

Foolish people are always fighting, but avoiding quarrels will bring you honor.
Proverbs 20:3 NCV

The fire of anger, if not quenched by loving forgiveness, will spread and defile and destroy the work of God.
Warren Wiersbe

Anger is the fluid that love bleeds when you cut it.
C. S. Lewis

Get rid of the poison of built-up anger and the acid of long-term resentment.
Charles Swindoll

MORE GOOD STUFF

Jealousy

Stop your anger! Turn from your rage!
Do not envy others—it only leads to harm.
Psalm 37:8 NLT

Too many Christians envy the sinners
their pleasures and the saints their joy,
because they don't have either one.
Martin Luther

What God asks, does, or requires of
others is not my business; it is His.
Kay Arthur

Discontent dries up the soul.
Elisabeth Elliot

2 MINUTES A DAY

Doubts

And immediately Jesus stretched forth
his hand, and caught him, and
said unto him, O thou of little faith,
wherefore didst thou doubt?
Matthew 14:31 KJV

Mark it down. God never turns away the
honest seeker. Go to God with
your questions. You may not find all
the answers, but in finding God,
you know the One who does.
Max Lucado

Doubting may temporarily disturb,
but will not permanently destroy,
your faith in Christ.
Charles Swindoll

MORE GOOD STUFF

Sin

Test all things; hold fast what is good.
Abstain from every form of evil.
1 Thessalonians 5:21, 22 NKJV

God is always ready to meet people
wherever they are, no matter how
dreadful their sins may seem.
Jim Cymbala

But suppose we do sin. Suppose we slip
and fall. Suppose we yield to temptation
for a moment. What happens?
We have to confess that sin.
Billy Graham

The holier a man becomes,
the more he mourns the unholiness
that remains in him.
C. H. Spurgeon

2 MINUTES A DAY

Temptation & Self-Control

No temptation has seized you except what is common to man. And God is faithful; he will not let you be tempted beyond what you can bear. But when you are tempted, he will also provide a way out so that you can stand up under it.

1 Corinthians 10:13 NIV

No trial is too great, no temptation is too strong, but that Jesus Christ can give us the mercy and the grace that we need, when we need it.

Warren Wiersbe

You have to say "yes" to God first before you can effectively say "no" to the devil.

Vance Havner

MORE GOOD STUFF

Judging Others

Judge not, and ye shall not be judged:
condemn not, and ye shall not be
condemned: forgive, and ye shall be
forgiven.
Luke 6:37 KJV

Judging draws the judgment of others.
Catherine Marshall

God loves these people too, just because
they're unattractive or warped in their
thinking doesn't mean the Lord doesn't
love them. And if we don't take them,
who is going to take them?
Ruth Bell Graham

When you extend hospitality to others, you're not trying to impress people, you're trying to reflect God to them.

Max Lucado

Promises

Perseverance

We are troubled on every side,
yet not distressed; we are perplexed,
but not in despair; Persecuted, but not
forsaken; cast down, but not destroyed.
2 Corinthians 4:8, 9 KJV

Every achievement worth remembering is
stained with the blood of diligence
and scarred by the wounds of
disappointment.
Charles Swindoll

Failure is one of life's most powerful
teachers. How we handle our failures
determines whether we're going to
simply "get by" in life or "press on."
Beth Moore

2 MINUTES A DAY

God never gives up on you, so don't you ever give up on Him.

Marie T. Freeman